KINGFISHER
READERS

Space

James Harrison

KINGFISHER
NEW YORK

KINGFISHER
LONDON & NEW YORK

Copyright © Macmillan Publishers International Ltd
Published in the United States by Kingfisher,
175 Fifth Ave., New York, NY 10010
Kingfisher is an imprint of Macmillan Children's Books, London.
All rights reserved.

Distributed in the U.S. and Canada by Macmillan,
175 Fifth Ave., New York, NY 10010

Library of Congress Cataloging-in-Publication data
has been applied for.

Series editor: Thea Feldman
Literacy consultant: Ellie Costa, Bank St. College, New York
Space consultant: Carole Stott

ISBN: 978-0-7534-6883-8 (HB)
ISBN: 978-0-7534-6884-5 (PB)

Kingfisher books are available for special promotions
and premiums. For details contact: Special Markets
Department, Macmillan, 175 Fifth Ave., New York, NY 10010.

For more information, please visit
www.kingfisherbooks.com

Printed in China
9 8 7 6 5
5TR/1115/UG/WKT/105MA

Picture credits
The Publisher would like to thank the following for permission to reproduce their material.
Every care has been taken to trace copyright holders.
(t = top, b = bottom, c = center, r = right, l = left):
Cover NASA/ESA, Science Photo Library (SPL)/Russell Croman, SPL/RIA Novosti, SPL/NASA;
Pages 4–5 SPL; 5tr SPL/Juliam Baum; 6–7c SPL/PLI; 9 Shutterstock/vovan; 11b Shutterstock/
oriontrail; 12t, 12b, 13 SPL/NASA; 16tr Nature PL/Eric Baccega; 16bl SPL//NASA; 21cl SPL/European
Southern Observatory; 21cr SPL/NASA/ESA/STSCi/Hubble; 21bl SPL/NOAO; 21br SPL/NASA/ESA/
STSCi; 22 SPL/Mehau Kulyk; 23c SPL/Russell Croman; 23br Shutterstock/Igor Chelkalin; 24 Getty/
Sandro Vannini/de Agostini; 25t SPL; 27t Shutterstock/Gunther Pichier; 27c Shutterstock/PRIMA;
28 SPL/John Sandford; 29cr SPL/Walter Pacholka/Astropics; 29bl Shutterstock/Kenneth V. Pilon;
30 European Southern Observatory; 31 Shutterstock; 32 SPL; 33t Shutterstock/MaszaS; 33b
Shutterstock/cbpix; 36 SPL/RIA Novosti; 37t SPL; 37b SPL/RIA Novosti; 42 SPL/NASA; 45t ISS/NASA.

Contents

What is space?

When you are outside on a clear night, look up at the sky. You are staring into space. You can see hundreds of twinkling stars. Gazing at the stars at night is the best way to understand how vast and distant space is.

Scientists called **astronomers** also look into space. They use powerful telescopes to learn more about space and the **universe**. We use the word universe to mean everything that exists, from our **planet**, Earth, to the most distant parts of space.

Earth from space

We have been able to see Earth from space for 50 years. Photos taken by **satellites** show us Earth as a blue ball with green and brown land covered by swirling white clouds.

Where does space start?

We are surrounded by a layer of air called the atmosphere. Imagine that Earth is an orange. The atmosphere is like the peel wrapped around the orange. There is no exact place where the atmosphere ends and space begins, but the top part of the atmosphere is about 60 miles (100 kilometers) above us .

Planet Earth

Earth is a planet in the **solar system**. It is the only planet in the solar system where there is life. There is oxygen in Earth's atmosphere, and there is water on the surface of Earth. We need both oxygen and water to survive.

In fact, Earth should really be called Water, because the oceans and seas cover two-thirds of the surface. That is why Earth looks mostly blue from space.

The inside of our planet is very different from the outside—inside it is so hot that rock melts.

How did Earth begin?

Scientists think that Earth formed as a ball of hot liquid rock 4.6 billion years ago. After millions more years, it had cooled down enough for solid rock to form the **crust**. This is the outer part where we live.

Inside Earth

Land and sea are
on the surface.

The center is
very hot.

The inside is rocky.

Earth's atmosphere
protects us from the
harmful rays of the Sun
and prevents Earth
from becoming too hot
or too cold. We are just
the right distance away
from the Sun for life
to exist.

A satellite photograph showing Earth
with deep blue oceans, white clouds,
and green-brown land masses

Night and day

Earth goes around the Sun along a path called an **orbit**. It takes one year—365 days—to complete an orbit.

While Earth moves along this path, it also spins around (like a spinning top) on an imaginary spike. The spike joins the North and South **poles** and is called the **axis**.

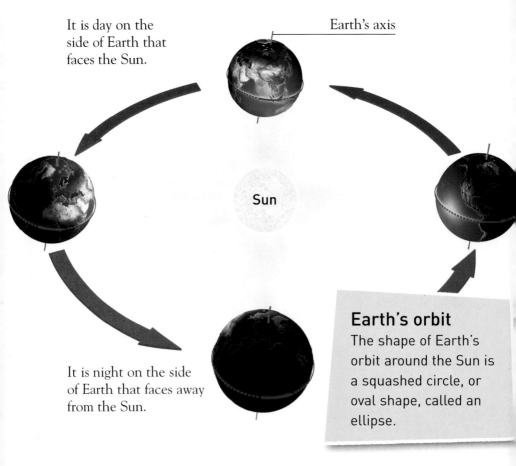

It is day on the side of Earth that faces the Sun.

Earth's axis

Sun

It is night on the side of Earth that faces away from the Sun.

Earth's orbit
The shape of Earth's orbit around the Sun is a squashed circle, or oval shape, called an ellipse.

Earth spins around on its axis once every 24 hours. The spinning gives us day (when the side that we are on faces the Sun) and night (when our side faces away from the Sun).

At dawn, it looks as if the Sun is rising above the horizon, but really it is Earth that is moving.

The Moon

The Moon moves around Earth. Like Earth, the Moon is made of rock, but it has no air, no water, and no life. It looks big because it is so close to us, but it is only one-fourth the size of Earth.

There are thousands of craters on the surface of the Moon.

The Moon is covered with **craters**—saucerlike dents up to 600 miles (1,000 kilometers) across. They were made by **meteorites** that have crashed into it over billions of years.

The Moon also has human footprints and vehicle tire tracks, made since humans first landed in 1969. It is the only place in the solar system that we have visited. The marks will be there for millions of years because there is no wind or weather to change the surface.

The Moon does not give off light of its own. The light we see is a **reflection** of some of the sunshine that falls on it.

The Moon orbits Earth
while they travel together
around the Sun.

Phases of the Moon

As the Moon orbits Earth, part or all of the side
facing Earth is lit by the Sun. This makes it look as
though the Moon changes shape from night to night.
This cycle takes 29.5 days, which is a lunar month.

Mars—the red planet

If you see a reddish-orange object
that looks like a star in the
night sky, it is probably the
planet Mars. It is called
the red planet because of
the color of the dust and
rocks on its surface.
Mars is named after
Mars, the Roman
god of war.

The biggest
volcano in the
solar system
is on Mars.
It is called
Olympus Mons.

Exploring Mars

Many unmanned **space probes** and space rovers have visited Mars and sent back pictures, but no human being has set foot on the planet—yet. Today, it would take about nine months to take a trip to Mars . . . and another nine months to come back again!

A space rover on Mars

Mars is a ball of rock with deserts, valleys, high mountains, and volcanoes. It also has seasons, as Earth does. A year on Mars is almost twice as long as an Earth year, but a day on Mars is about the same length as a day on Earth. The temperature on Mars is much, much colder than it is on Earth.

The giant planets

Four of the planets in our solar system look like giant balls of gas from Earth. When we look at Jupiter, Saturn, Uranus, and Neptune, we see the tops of their thick atmospheres. Deep inside, all of the planets have a rocky **core**.

Jupiter is the biggest planet in our solar system, and it could swallow up more than 1,300 Earths. It spins around so fast that it creates colored bands of clouds. One of these is a giant cloud called the

Jupiter
The surface of Jupiter is always changing.

Great Red Spot

Saturn
Saturn has 62 satellites orbiting around it, but more are being discovered.

Great Red Spot. This is a massive moving storm that has been raging for more than 300 years.

All of the giant planets have rings around them, and Saturn's rings are the most extensive. Saturn's rings are made of countless pieces of ice, rock, and dust.

Uranus and Neptune are similar to each other, but Uranus is tilted on its side. Both of these planets are about four times bigger than Earth.

Uranus
Uranus was the first planet to be discovered after the telescope was invented.

Neptune
Neptune is the farthest planet from the Sun.

Here comes the Sun

For everyone who lives on planet Earth, the Sun is special. But, the Sun is just an ordinary star—no bigger or shinier than others you see on a starry night. It looks bigger because it is closer than other stars—93 million miles (150 million kilometers) away. The Sun is our local star. This huge fireball gives us all of our light and warmth, and without it there would be no life.

How big?
You could fit 109 Earths side by side across the width of the Sun.

Huge clouds of gas flare up from the surface of the Sun.

The temperature at
the surface of the Sun
is about 10,000°F
(5,500°C).

Core

Surface

Close-up pictures show that the Sun
looks like a bubbling cauldron as
hot gases rush out. Some huge
flares of gas leap up so far that
they completely escape. The
temperatures are so high that
at its core (center) the Sun
makes **nuclear energy**, and
this makes it shine.

All living things depend on the Sun's energy.
Plants use it to grow, and animals, including
people, rely on plants for energy.

The solar system

Earth is always moving around the Sun, along with other planets and smaller objects such as moons, **comets**, and **asteroids**. The Sun and everything traveling around it make up the solar system. The word *solar* means "of the Sun."

All of these objects travel together along orbits around the Sun because of the pull of the Sun's **gravity**. The farther away a planet is from the Sun, the longer it takes to orbit (go around) it. Mercury is the closest planet, and it takes 88 days to orbit the Sun. Earth takes 365 days, and Neptune takes more than 60,000 days!

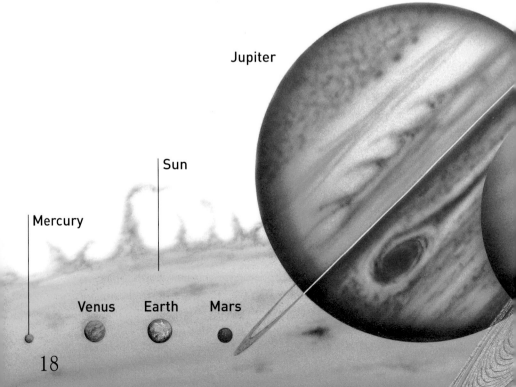

Jupiter

Sun

Mercury

Venus   Earth   Mars

The solar system is vast. It is so big that it takes eight minutes for the Sun's light to reach Earth. The spaces between the planets are huge compared with their sizes. Imagine that you are holding a soccerball. If the Sun were the size of the soccerball, Earth would be only half the size of a pea and almost 82 feet (25 meters) away!

From biggest to smallest
The planets Jupiter, Saturn, Uranus, and Neptune are much bigger than Earth, but Venus, Mars, and Mercury are smaller.

Saturn

Uranus

Neptune

Our home galaxy

Planet Earth is important to us, but it is just a little planet going around the Sun. The Sun is just one of a big group of stars called a **galaxy**. Our galaxy contains billions of stars and is called the Milky Way.

If you could travel out into space and look back, you would see that our galaxy is shaped like a flat disc with a bulge in the middle. Our solar system is far away from the center.

Our Solar System

Earth and our solar system are a tiny part of the barred spiral galaxy called the Milky Way. All of the stars we see at night are in the Milky Way.

Wherever you are on Earth, you should be able to see parts of the Milky Way in the night sky. Try looking for it on a very dark, clear night. If you have a telescope or binoculars, you will see thousands of faint stars.

Galaxy shapes

Galaxies have different shapes. Some have **spiral** arms coming out of a circle. Some have spiral arms around a bar shape. Some are elliptical (egg shaped) and a few are irregular (uneven) shapes.

Spiral galaxy

Barred spiral galaxy

Elliptical galaxy

Irregular galaxy

The universe

Universe is a word we use to describe everything that exists. This means everything we can see around us and also everything above us in the sky—our Moon, our Sun, and our solar system. Beyond that lies our galaxy, the Milky Way. Even farther out are many more distant galaxies.

The big bang
Scientists know that our universe is growing and cooling at the same time. They think that the universe began as an explosion called the **big bang**. After the big bang, space was stretched out—imagine a balloon being blown up—over millions of years. At the same time, the stars and planets were forming. The whole universe is still expanding.

The universe is made up of three basic things. There is ordinary **matter**, which makes the planets, stars and galaxies, and other things we can see or measure. There is dark matter, a mysterious invisible mass found between the stars and galaxies. And there is dark energy, another invisible ingredient that scientists still do not understand.

This dark cloud of dust and gas is called the Horsehead Nebula. Can you see why?

This is the Andromeda galaxy. It is the closest large galaxy to the Milky Way.

The sky at night

Remember the song *Twinkle, Twinkle, Little Star?* The stars seem to twinkle when you look up at them on a dark, clear night. This is because we look up through air that is always moving around, so the starlight is unsteady, making the stars seem to twinkle. If you could see a star from a spacecraft, it would shine steadily.

These stars were painted in a tomb in ancient Egypt thousands of years ago.

Since ancient times, people have looked at the stars and grouped them into shapes and patterns called **constellations**. The outlines were often based on old stories about people or animals such as a bull or crab. Ancient Greek, Arab, and Chinese astronomers all gave names to the groups of stars they could see.

This picture shows astronomers investigating the sky hundreds of years ago in a place called Galata, now part of modern-day Turkey.

The constellation Pegasus was named after a winged horse in ancient Greek mythology.

What is a star?

A star is an enormous spinning ball of hot, bright gases. The changing gases produce a lot of energy. Scientists call this nuclear energy, and it is what makes stars shine.

A star starts as a ball of gas and dust that is pulled together strongly by gravity. The gas and dust get warmer and more squashed until the gas is so hot that nuclear energy is made. Then a star is born.

Stars are different colors because some are hotter than others. Cooler stars are redder, and hotter stars look more bluish-white.

The life of a star

Stars begin life in a huge spinning cloud of gas and dust.

A part of the cloud comes together to make a star.

Billions of years later, toward the end of their lives, stars like our Sun become 100 times bigger.

Changing colors

When we heat a piece of metal, the colors change. The metal glows red hot, then becomes brighter and more yellow until it is white hot. Stars shine in the same way depending on how hot they are.

When it has used up all of the gas inside it, a star pushes away its outer layer and its core shrinks.

Our Sun is a middle-aged star. Today it is classified as a yellow star. In about five billion years, it will run out of gas and start to cool down.

Most stars then cool down and die.

Meteors

You can see many other objects in space on a clear night. You might see a point of light suddenly dart across the night sky. We call this a shooting star, but it is not a star at all—it is a meteor.

Barringer Crater, Arizona is 0.75 miles (1.2 kilometers) across.

This piece of meteorite weighs 1.3 oz. (37g) and was traveling at 45 mi. (72km) per second when it hit the ground in Arizona.

Meteor showers

As Earth travels around the Sun, it sometimes goes through a stream of space dust. When this happens, we see meteor showers. These are spectacular groups of shooting stars.

Meteors streak across the sky.

A meteor is a streak of light made by a tiny piece of space rock or dust speeding through Earth's atmosphere.

Most of these tiny pieces of space rock burn up in Earth's atmosphere. Some bigger pieces get through and hit land or water really hard. These lumps of rock are called meteorites. Some are big enough to make craters (like the craters on the Moon). The most famous crater on Earth is in Arizona. It was made more than 50,000 years ago and measures 0.75 miles (1.2 kilometers) across.

Comets

Comets are big chunks of snow and dust. There are millions of comets far out in space beyond the planets. Occasionally one travels toward the Sun and, as it gets close, it starts to melt and turn into gas. Pieces of dust break off from the comet, and the gas and dust form a huge head and tails. A comet has two tails—one of gas and another of dust. The tails can be millions of miles long, and they always point away from the Sun.

This comet, Hale-Bopp, was last visible in 1997. You can see its two tails.

Halley's comet

Halley's comet was named after Edmund Halley.
He saw it in 1682 and was the first person to
realize that it was a regular visitor. Chinese
astronomers had seen it 2,000 years before that.

Halley's comet was woven into the Bayeux Tapestry, a very old cloth
that tells the story of the Battle of Hastings in England in 1066.

Some comets travel toward the Sun, then move off into
space and disappear. Others go around the Sun in long
oval orbits. The most famous is Halley's comet, which we
can see from Earth every 75 to 76 years. The last time it
passed was in 1986, and it is next expected in 2061.

Studying space

The study of objects in space is called astronomy. Astronomers have studied the stars and estimated their sizes and distances from us in space since ancient times. During the 1500s, an astronomer named Copernicus showed that the Sun was in the center of the solar system, with the planets orbiting around it. Before then, people believed that Earth was in the center of the universe.

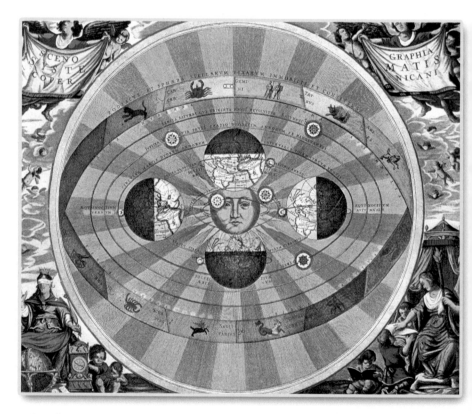

This diagram shows the astronomer Copernicus's idea that the Sun is in the center of the solar system.

Studying space

Telescopes use lenses or mirrors to gather and focus the light from far away objects. This makes it easier to study outer space in detail.

In the early 1600s, Galileo became the first person to use a telescope to look at the Sun, Moon, and planets. His telescopes showed him the Moon's craters and mountains, as well as spots on the Sun's surface, four Moons around Jupiter, and many more stars. Galileo's telescopes made a huge difference to astronomy.

Radio telescopes have large metal dishes. Sometimes they are grouped together to gather more signals from space.

Space probes

Unmanned spacecraft sent out to explore our solar system are usually called space probes. They carry powerful cameras and sensors to record what they see. There have been around 40 missions to Mars that have flown near or landed on that planet. Not all of them have been able to send back information; some of the probes have crashed or have lost contact with Earth.

Other space probes have orbited the Sun's poles, flown past comets, and landed on asteroids.

The Hubble Space Telescope was launched in April 1990 and orbits Earth around 350 miles (570 kilometers) above us.

In 2004, the space probe *Cassini* reached Saturn and sent back photographs of the planet's rings.

Pioneer 10 was the first space probe to fly close to Jupiter. In 2003, after 30 years of flying, it sent back its final signal. It continues its long journey in silence as it flies toward a red star called Aldebaran.

Space telescopes study space from above our atmosphere and send back beautifully clear photos, as well as **x-ray**, **ultraviolet**, and **infrared** pictures.

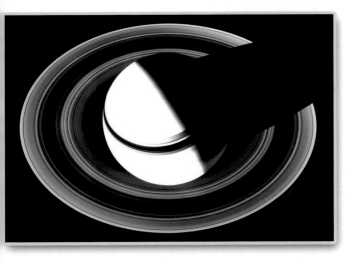

This photo of Saturn and its rings was taken by *Cassini*. The rings around Saturn are made of ice, rock, and dust.

The race for space

The space age began in 1957, when the Soviet Union (now Russia) launched the first satellite—*Sputnik 1*. It orbited Earth for 98 minutes. It was the size of a beach ball and was made of light metal with four **antennae**. A month later, *Sputnik 2* carried the first dog to orbit Earth. Her name, Laika, means "barker" in Russian.

In 1961, the Soviet spacecraft *Vostok 1* carried Yuri Gagarin into orbit. He was the first man in space and spent 108 minutes there.

Laika inside a model of her space cabin

The United States launched its space program with the Mercury space missions and, later, the Gemini and Apollo missions. One month after Yuri Gagarin's trip, Alan Shepard became the first American in space.

Today people from many other countries, including China and Japan, have gone into space. Several countries worked together on the International **Space Station**, the biggest structure ever built in space.

Alan Shepard blasts off in 1961.

Space firsts

First satellite in space
Sputnik 1: October 4, 1957

First animal to orbit Earth
Laika on *Sputnik 2*:
November 3, 1957

First man in space
Soviet Yuri Gagarin
(*Vostok 1*): April 12, 1961

First woman in space
Soviet Valentina Tereshkova
(*Vostok 6*): June 16, 1963

First walk in space unattached to craft
American Bruce McCandless II (*Challenger*):
February 7, 1984

Valentina Tereshkova

Man on the Moon

On July 20, 1969, at 10:56 P.M. EDT, astronaut Neil Armstrong said, "That's one small step for man, one giant leap for mankind." He had become the first human being to step onto the surface of the Moon.

Following Armstrong down the steps of the *Apollo 11* **lunar module** was fellow astronaut Buzz Aldrin. Together they took photographs, set up television cameras, planted a flag, and collected Moon rocks.

More than 600 million people watched on television as the astronauts walked and hopped over the surface. On the Moon, a person can jump six times as high as on Earth because the Moon's gravity is weaker.

When the astronauts took off their helmets later, they described a strong smell like wet ashes in a fireplace. It was the Moon dust on their boots.

Every step the astronauts took threw up fine dust.

Apollo missions

Twelve American astronauts landed on
the Moon from 1969 to 1972 in six Apollo
missions. They spent 80 hours taking
photographs, collecting samples, and
driving a Moon car called a lunar rover.
No one has been on the Moon since 1972.

Space shuttle

The United States' space shuttle was the first space plane. It was made up of three parts: the orbiter, the solid rocket boosters, and the external tank. It flew into space more than 130 times.

The orbiter was the size of a short-range airliner, with a flight cabin at the front and, behind this, an area for eating, sleeping, and working. In another section, it could carry space probes, telescopes, repair equipment, and parts to build space stations.

The space shuttle lifted off from Earth like a rocket, and the orbiter returned like a glider plane.

Orbiter

Wings

Tail fin

External tank

Two solid rocket boosters helped blast the orbiter into space. They fell away into the ocean and were found by ships. The only part not reused was the external tank, which was discarded once the fuel inside it was used up. The orbiter operated as a spacecraft in orbit around Earth until it reentered the atmosphere and landed on a runway, like a plane. A large parachute opened on landing to act as a brake.

Solid rocket booster

The need for speed

To reach space we have to escape from the pull of gravity—the force that holds us down on Earth. The space shuttle reached a speed of more than 17,500 miles (28,000 kilometers) per hour to get into orbit.

How to be an astronaut

Thousands of people apply to be an astronaut.
If you are chosen, you have to train very hard for
at least a year before you can go on a space flight.

All sorts of men and women become astronauts.
Many have studied science subjects in college.

All the parts of a space
suit lock together so
that the air inside
cannot escape.

An astronaut
puts on her
spacesuit and
backpack.

Japanese astronauts float around in a special aircraft, nicknamed the "Vomit Comet" to feel what it is like to be weightless.

Space agencies are looking for doctors, biologists, geologists, engineers, and people who have worked in the armed forces, especially pilots.

Astronauts need to learn a lot about space flight and spacecraft, and they need to be in very good shape. They train in mock spaceships inside giant water tanks and take rides in a diving airplane to feel what it is like to be weightless, as they will be in space. They learn how to work in bulky spacesuits and how to land with a parachute on land or in the ocean.

Space stations

A space station is a home in space. Astronauts onboard live, work, and sleep as the station orbits around Earth.

Astronauts do not wear spacesuits inside the space station. The cabins hold air to breathe and protect the crew from harmful rays and dust. The biggest problem is weightlessness. Everything floats, including the astronauts, so they are strapped down to sleep, and their food is strapped to their eating trays.

The International Space Station (ISS) is so large that we can see it at night from Earth. People can live on the ISS for many months at a time. Supplies and relief crews come aboard in a spacecraft that docks or links with the station. Many different crews have lived onboard over the past ten years.

Flight engineers on the International Space Station make lunch.

A free-floating astronaut tries to catch his pen, and another is strapped down while he sleeps. Two others float and spin.

Going to the bathroom in space
Astronauts use a special toilet that stops liquid and solid waste from floating away. A fan sucks everything into the toilet.

Glossary

antennae devices that send out and receive radio, TV, and satellite signals

asteroids small, rocky bodies that orbit the Sun

astronomers people who study the stars, planets, and other bodies in space

axis an imaginary line through the center of an object, around which the object spins

big bang the massive explosion that scientists think created the universe

comets balls of frozen snow and dust that travel around the Sun

constellations patterns of bright stars that people have imagined to help us spot and identify stars

core the very hot center of a planet or star

craters bowl-shaped holes made by a crashing object

crust the surface layer of a rocky planet or moon

flares exploding hot gases on the outer layer of the Sun

galaxy a group of stars, planets, dust, and gas kept together by gravity

gravity the force that pulls one thing toward another

infrared a type of light ray outside the range of visible light that lets us see things using heat energy

lunar module the landing craft that took astronauts to the Moon's surface

matter anything that takes up space

meteorites rock or metal pieces from space that reach the surface of Earth without breaking up

nuclear energy a source of power that is released when the structure of atoms is altered

orbit to travel around another object in space; *also* the path of an object in space around another

planet a large, round body made of rock or gas that orbits a star

poles the points furthest north and furthest south of Earth through which the axis passes

reflection light, heat, or sound bouncing back from a surface

satellites objects orbiting a planet. Satellites are natural, such as moons, or human-made, such as space telescopes

solar system the Sun and everything that orbits it

space probes unmanned spacecraft sent from Earth to explore the solar system

space station a spacecraft big enough for people to live and work on

spiral a type of galaxy in the shape of a pinwheel

ultraviolet a type of light ray with short wave lengths outside the range of visible light

universe all of space and everything it contains

x-ray a powerful wave of energy that helps us see through some objects

Index